# Spellathon
## Book 4

www.pegasusforkids.com

**© B. Jain Publishers (P) Ltd.** All rights reserved. No part of this book may be reproduced, stored in a retrieval system or transmitted, in any form or by any means, mechanical, photocopying, recording or otherwise, without any prior written permission of the publisher.

Published by Kuldeep Jain for B. Jain Publishers (P) Ltd., D-157, Sector 63, Noida - 201307, U.P.
Registered office: 1921/10, Chuna Mandi, Paharganj, New Delhi-110055

Printed in India

# CONTENTS

A, B AND C ............................................................. 4

D, E AND F ............................................................. 7

G, H AND I ............................................................. 11

J, K AND L ............................................................. 14

M, N AND O ............................................................. 17

P, Q AND R ............................................................. 20

S, T AND U ............................................................. 23

V, W AND X ............................................................. 26

U, V AND W ............................................................. 26

Y AND Z ............................................................. 28

EXERCISES ............................................................. 31

APPENDIX: SIGHT WORDS ............................................................. 34

ANSWERS ............................................................. 35

# A, B AND C

1. Name the following by filling in the blanks:

   a.

   B _ _ k _ t

   b.

   _ a _ _ o _

   c.

   B _ c _ cl _

   d.

   A _ _ rd

   e.

   _ r _ _ d

   f.

   Ch _ m _ le _

   g.

   A _ ch _ r

   h.

   Ca _ e _ p _ ll _ r

   i.

   _ nt _ l _ pe

2. One word in each sentence is incorrect. Correct the wrong words:

   a. Hema liked the blak dress better than the green one.
   b. The man was very charmeng.
   c. The magician was really ameizing.
   d. Sue is constuntly hungry.
   e. A thief is also called a burgler.
   f. I am very good at addition.

Date: _____        Teacher's Signature: _____

Write the plural of the following:

a. Bone       _____
b. Child      _____
c. Animal     _____
d. Brother    _____
e. Aunt       _____
f. Cherry     _____

Rearrange the jumbled letters to find the correct words:

| Basket   Camping   Aching   Bamboo   Archer   Circle   Branches |

a. The tree had many _____. (bnrahcse)
b. The girl was spinning in a _____. (cricel)
c. Pandas love to eat _____ shoots. (mbaobo)
d. The girl was making a _____ out of straw. (bkatse)
e. An _____ uses bow and arrow to shoot at a target. (rahecr)
f. I hurt my knee and it is now _____. (agnich)
g. My friends and I love sleeping in a tent when we go _____. (cmpanig)

Change a letter in each word to make a new word. Remember, you can use either a, b, or c:

a. BATTLE      _ ATTLE
b. GRAIN       _ RAIN
c. FLOG        FL _ G
d. DRAG        DRA _
e. LURE        _ URE
f. SWORE       _ W _ RE

Teacher's Signature: _____         Date: _____

6. Say the following sentence aloud as fast as you can, and as many times as you can!

   "Betty bought some pots of butter, but she said the butter's bitter, so she bought some better butter to make the bitter butter better."

## Words to Remember

**A** Ache, Aching, Actor, Addition, Aeroplane, Afraid, After, Agile, Album, Alligator, Always, Amazing, Anchor, Angel, Angry, Animal, Ankle, Annoy, Ant, Antelope, Apartment, Apple, Aquarium, Archer, Artist, Ash, Atlas, Attire, August, Aunt, Autumn, Award, Aware, Axis

**B** Bail, Balloon, Bamboo, Bandit, Bangle, Barter, Base, Basket, Bear, Being, Better, Bile, Birth, Birthday, Bitter, Black, Blame, Bland, Boat, Boil, Bone, Bottle, Bow, Boyhood, Brain, Branch, Bread, Break, Bring, Brother, Buffalo, Bungle, Burgle, Bus, Business, Butter, Butterfly

**C** Cage, Calf, Carrot, Caterpillar, Caught, Cave, Charming, Cherry, Child, Children, Circle, Circus, Claim, Classic, Claw, Clay, Clear, Clown, Coal, Cocoon, Compare, Consume, Cow, Cradle, Crane, Crate, Cream, Create, Cripple, Crop, Cross, Crow, Cub, Cup, Curtain

Date: _____                                     Teacher's Signature: _____

# D, E AND F

1. Look at the pictures and choose the correct spellings:

a. Dragun
   Dragon
   Dragine

b. Elephant
   Elifant
   Elephent

c. Flamenco
   Flamengu
   Flamingo

d. Flour
   Floawer
   Flower

e. Dynoseros
   Dinousar
   Dinosaur

f. Eighteen
   Eiteen
   Eightine

g. Drame
   Drome
   Drum

h. Exercise
   Exercize
   Excersize

i. Framing
   Farming
   Farmeing

j. Dreem
   Dreme
   Dream

Teacher's Signature: _____
Date: _____

2. Use the first letters of the names of the following to make new words:

   a. dog + ant + girl + goat + ear + rainbow = _____

   b. fish + leaf + gorilla + monkey + elephant = _____

   c. egg + apple + rabbit + lion + yo-yo = _____

   d. drum + arrow + nose + chilli + eye = _____

   e. hawk + nail + grapes + leaf + ice cream + star + hand = _____

   f. flower + ostrich + knot + crab + egg = _____

3. Unscramble the words using the hints given below:

   a. NUDGOEN          _____
      (Hint: A place where prisoners were kept in a castle)

   b. ERGAE            _____
      (Hint: To look forward to something keenly)

   c. GORFET           _____
      (Hint: Not remember)

   d. FCORTYA          _____
      (Hint: A place where things are made)

   e. EALDET           _____
      (Hint: Very happy)

Date: _____                                Teacher's Signature: _____

f. LIDUNCKG _____
   (Hint: A baby duck)

g. DGDOE _____
   (Hint: To avoid)

h. ECSPAE _____
   (Hint: To run away from somewhere)

i. MFAOSU _____
   (Hint: Well known)

j. RFALI _____
   (Hint: Weak and small)

> Escape     Duckling    Famous     Dodge     Frail
> Elated     Factory     Dungeon    Forget    Eager

Make sentences using the following words:

a. Dance _____

b. Farmer _____

c. Easy _____

d. From _____

e. Drawing _____

f. Energy _____

Tick (✓) the correct words:

a. A (deer/dear) runs very fast.

b. We see with our (ears/eyes).

c. We (drink/draw) with a pencil.

d. We have two (foot/feet).

e. Saturday comes after (Sunday/Friday).

Teacher's Signature: _____          Date: _____

f. Birds of a (feather/further) flock together.

g. We have a lot of (engage/energy) in the morning.

h. I cannot swim, but I can (flout/float) in the water.

i. The boats were tied up at the (dock/draft).

j. Sadness and happiness are opposite (ethnic/emotions).

6. How many words can you make using the word given below?

   EVERYONE

   _____   _____   _____   _____

   _____   _____   _____   _____

   _____   _____   _____   _____

   _____   _____   _____   _____

   _____   _____   _____   _____

**Words to Remember**

**D** Dagger, Dancer, Dapper, Darkness, Dart, Dawn, Daze, Deaf, Deafening, Dear, Debt, Deck, Deer, Dirty, Dock, Dome, Doubt, Dove, Draft, Drawing, Drawl, Dribble, Drift, Drinking, Dripping, Drive, Drop, Drown, Drum, Ducklings, Dungeon

**E** Each, Eager, Eager, Eagle, Ears, Eastern, Easy, Eating, Ebony, Echo, Edit, Effect, Effort, Eggs, Eighty, Elephant, Elongate, Embarrass, Emotion, Enact, Ending, Energy, Engage, Enough, Eon, Erupt, Etch, Ethnic, Evening, Everyone, Everything, Excited, Eyes

**F** Fable, Face, Faded, Fairy, Famous, Fancy, Feast, Feet, Festival, Fidget, Fishing, Flaming, Flamingo, Flavour, Fleece, Flight, Float, Floor, Flowers, Flying, Foam, Focus, Fond, Foot, Forget, Forward, Found, Freckle, Friday, Frightened, Frigid, Frogs, Fumble

Date: _____                              Teacher's Signature: _____

# G, H AND I

1. Name the following animals, and circle the ones you would find on a farm:

| Goat  | Giraffe | Hippopotamus | Horse   | Hen |
| Goose | Gorilla | Golden Eagle | Gazelle |     |

2. Sometimes, we write two words together in a shortened form. Write the full form of the following words. The first one has been done for you:

   a. I'll: <u>I will</u>   b. I'm: _____   c. It's: _____

   d. I'd: _____   e. I've: _____   f. It'll: _____

3. Write the Past Tense of the following words:

   a. Grow _____   b. Hear _____   c. Give _____

   d. Help _____   e. Grasp _____   f. Get _____

   g. Infer _____   h. Greet _____   i. Imply _____

Teacher's Signature: _____   Date: _____

4. Look at the pictures and fill in the blanks:

   a. _____ and _____ are fruits.

   b. An _____ is made of blocks of ice.

   c. A _____ like to eat _____.

5. Find the following words in the Word Grid:

   | Giraffe | Height | Hassle | Hanker |
   | Hefty | Grocery | Genuine | Inland |
   | Island | Icicle | Igloo | Ignore |
   | Impish | Injure | Hedge | Habitable |

   | I | G | L | O | O | G | I | L | T | E | N | G |
   |---|---|---|---|---|---|---|---|---|---|---|---|
   | H | N | E | I | S | L | A | N | D | T | E | R |
   | S | U | J | L | G | T | S | R | L | I | S | O |
   | G | E | N | U | I | N | E | G | L | A | E | W |
   | E | I | A | P | R | D | O | U | P | I | N | L |
   | H | A | S | S | L | E | F | R | E | C | C | D |
   | A | O | L | E | H | E | D | G | E | I | I | G |
   | H | A | B | I | T | A | B | L | E | C | M | L |
   | E | C | H | A | N | K | E | R | E | L | P | E |
   | F | G | R | O | C | E | R | Y | K | E | I | A |
   | T | G | I | R | A | F | F | E | E | C | S | M |
   | Y | G | E | S | T | U | H | E | I | G | H | T |

Date: _____     Teacher's Signature: _____

5. Read the passage and choose the right words to fill in the blanks:

Shama was very _____ (hangry/hungry) so she went _____ (onto/into) the kitchen. She thought, "Maybe I can eat some _____ (ice cream/ice crame)." But there was none in the freezer.

So she thought, "I could have some _____ (haught/hot) chocolate." But she could not find any milk.

"Maybe _____ (I've/I'll) have to stay hungry," she thought. Just then her stomach made a loud _____ (grumbling/gambling) noise. Luckily, her mother came _____ (house/home) and said, "Shama, come and eat this sandwich I _____ (got/goat) for you."

Shama was very _____ (greatful/grateful) and thanked her mother.

## Words to Remember

**G** Game, Gemini, Genuine, Get, Ghost, Gifted, Giraffe, Girth, Gleam, Glint, Goat, Golden, Goose, Gorilla, Government, Grade, Grandfather, Grandmother, Grant, Grapes, Graph, Grasp, Grass, Grateful, Grave, Graze, Great, Grew, Grow, Growing, Growl, Gruff, Grumpy, Guava

**H** Hair, Hamper, Handsome, Happily, Hear, Heave, Hedge, Heed, Hefty, Helicopter, Help, Hem, Hen, Hence, Hive, Hoarse, Hopeful, Hopping, Horse, Hosted, Hound, House, Hover, Howl, Hundred, Hurl, Hurt, Hush, Hymn,

**I** I'd, I'll, I'm, I've, Iceland, Icicle, Idiotic, Igloo, Ill, Imply, Income, Inland, Insist, Irate, Island, It's, Itch

# J, K AND L

1. The following words have been jumbled. Find the words with the help of the hints:

   a. JRUY　　　＿＿＿＿＿＿＿＿
   (Hint: A group of people who help a judge decide cases)

   b. KCIKDE　　＿＿＿＿＿＿＿＿
   (Hint: Hit with the foot)

   c. JKOUBEX　＿＿＿＿＿＿＿＿
   (Hint: A large music player)

   d. KFIEN　　＿＿＿＿＿＿＿＿
   (Hint: A sharp tool used to cut things)

   e. NUJAAYR　＿＿＿＿＿＿＿＿
   (Hint: The first month of the year)

   f. TKIHCEN　＿＿＿＿＿＿＿＿
   (Hint: Place where food is cooked)

   g. TRLETE　　＿＿＿＿＿＿＿＿
   (Hint: A piece of paper with a message on it)

2. Choose the right words to fill in the blanks:

   a. I am ＿＿＿＿＿＿ (keen/kine) to watch the new movie.
   b. The girl was ＿＿＿＿＿＿ (locky/lucky) to find her lost wallet.
   c. Fred was ＿＿＿＿＿＿ (jousting/joking) that he had won the ＿＿＿＿＿＿ (lottery/loot).
   d. Rosy enjoyed ＿＿＿＿＿＿ (jazz/jose) music.
   e. Jill worked ＿＿＿＿＿＿ (linger/longer) than Jack.
   f. There was no ＿＿＿＿＿＿ (lable/label) on the box.

Date: ＿＿＿＿＿＿　　　　　　　　　　　　　　Teacher's Signature: ＿＿＿＿＿＿

3. Correct the following sentences:

   a. Dan jamped over the bush.
   _____

   b. The rope was tied up in nots.
   _____

   c. She is the keindest person I know.
   _____

   d. The boys new how to knit.
   _____

   e. Roy bought two loves of bread.
   _____

   f. There were no leafes on the tree.
   _____

   g. The tiger is the king of the jangle.
   _____

   h. The loyer presents cases to the judg in court.
   _____

4. Change an alphabet to make new words:

   a. BARD            BAR __
   b. DOVE            __ OVE
   c. INSURE          IN __ URE
   d. PANTRY          PA __ TRY
   e. BANTER          BAN __ ER
   f. LINE            LIN __
   g. POKER           __ OKER
   h. CHORE           CHO __ E

Teacher's Signature: _____                    Date: _____

5. Write the plural of the following words:

   a. Leaf        _____

   b. Knife       _____

   c. Lady        _____

   d. Jungle      _____

   e. Kitten      _____

   f. Jail        _____

### Words to Remember

**J** — Jug, Jungle, January, Jingle, Jostle, Joyous, Joking, Jumping, Jail, Jazz, Jamb, Jovial, Judge, Jukebox, Jaw, Jewel, Juice, Jute, Jeans

**K** — Kitten, Kitchen, Know, Key, Kilt, Kibble, Keen, Kinder, Kissed, Kicked, Knave, Knotted, Knitted, Knew, Knee, Kangaroo, Kite, Karate, Kiwi, Kneel, Knight

**L** — Leaf, Letter, Learnt, Large, Larger, Largest, Lift, Loaves, Longer, Label, Lawyer, Lick, Lumber, Ladder, Liar, Lever, Lunch, Leopard, Leather, Lively, Laugh, Linger, Layer

Date: _____        Teacher's Signature: _____

# M, N AND O

Name the following:

a.  __ AG __ CIA __

b.  __ A __ HE __ ATI __ S

c.  __ ST __ IC __

d.  __ AP __ I __

e.  __ XE __

f.  __ O __ KE __

g.  __ EIG __ BOU __

h.  __ IG __ T

Choose the correct spellings:

a. The horse _____ (neighed/neither/nought) when he saw his rider.

b. Fanny _____ (overthought/overheard/oval) two boys talking.

c. Percy had a pet _____ (oul /oil/owl).

Teacher's Signature: _____   Date: _____

d. The tiny ant defeated the _____ (nightly/mighty/mouthy) elephant

e. It was raining so we couldn't play _____ (outside/other/overt).

f. The _____ (mankeys/monikers/monkeys) in the zoo were very _____ (noisy/nosy/norse).

g. The pet parrot was sad because its _____ (owner/opener/oinker) _____ (niggle/ neglected/nuanced) it.

3. Fill in the blanks:

| Music | November | O'clock | Maximum |
| Nose | Money | Orange | |

a. _____ comes before December.

b. My father keeps his _____ in his wallet.

c. I like to listen to _____.

d. I go to sleep at nine _____.

e. I smell with my _____.

f. My favourite fruit is the _____.

g. The pilot flew the aircraft at _____ speed.

4. Match the following to make new compound words:

a. Over         stick

b. News         man

c. Match         pad

d. Milk         land

e. Night         paper

f. Mega         time

g. Main         come

h. Note         phone

Date: _____         Teacher's Signature: _____

5. Where is the owl?

The owl is

sitting _____ a branch,

flying _____ the tree.

_____ the tree.

## Words to Remember

**M** Music, Money, Mouse, Mouth, Man, Milkman, Matchstick, Mainland, Mining, Mint, Mango, Miniature, Magazine, Male, Mail, Make, Magic, Magician, Major, Market, Merit, Modern, Mother, Mould, Munch, Maximum, Minimum, Movie, Morsel

**N** Nose, November, Nest, Near, Newspaper, Night-Time, Nasty, Noisy, Never, Nearly, New, Number, Nice, Navy, Nail, Nineteen, Nervous, Nobody, North, Nothing

**O** O'clock, Orange, On, Over, Ox, Outside, Other, Often, Overcome, Officer, Ocean, Ostrich, Oak, Older, Oats, October, Owner

Teacher's Signature: _____     Date: _____

# P, Q AND R

1. Each of the following are missing letter. It could be p, q or r. Fill in the missing letters:

    a. Al_ha  _____    b. Ac_uire  _____

    c. T_eat  _____    d. _uill  _____

    e. Tende_  _____   f. S_ort  _____

    g. A_mour  _____   h. Mo_al  _____

2. Match the picture to the action:

    a.              playing

    b.              riding

    c.              running

    d.              reading

    e.              painting

3. Fill in the blanks:

    | River | Quilt | Ready | Pair | Quiet |
    | People | Queue | Pass | Plastic | Reward |

    a. I have a _____ of black shoes.

    b. Can you _____ me the salt?

c. We must stand in a _____ at the bus stop.
d. Are you _____? We will be late for school.
e. Many _____ are going to see the circus.
f. There is a boat on the _____.
g. We should not use _____ bags.
h. All the children were _____ during morning prayers.
i. It was cold, so Joe slept under a warm _____.
j. The brave boy was given a _____ by the President.

4. Unscramble the jumbled words and find them in the word grid:

   a. A white, round gem that is formed inside an oyster — RPEAL
   b. To argue with someone — QARURLE
   c. Happening again and again — PREEADET
   d. To think of something that happened earlier — MEREMREB
   e. A green bird that can talk — RAPROT
   f. To give up — UQTI
   g. Nice looking — RETPYT
   h. An army division — PALTNOO
   i. Strange — QEURE
   j. A member of the cat family — PTHANER
   k. Case in which arrows are kept — VUIQER
   l. Santa Claus' sled is pulled by _____ — RINEREDE
   m. Not smooth — GHRUO
   n. Thief — BORBRE
   o. Sound made by ducks — KQUCA

Teacher's Signature: _____          Date: _____

| | | | | | | | | | | |
|---|---|---|---|---|---|---|---|---|---|---|
| E | D | Q | T | P | A | R | R | O | T | |
| L | E | O | Q | U | I | V | E | R | U | |
| Q | Q | U | A | C | K | U | I | Q | Q | |
| P | P | L | A | T | O | O | N | U | U | |
| R | E | P | E | A | T | E | D | A | E | |
| E | R | E | M | E | M | B | E | R | E | |
| T | O | P | A | N | T | H | E | R | R | |
| T | U | R | O | B | B | E | R | E | P | |
| Y | G | R | A | P | E | A | R | L | T | |
| R | H | E | O | Q | U | I | T | G | O | |

| Quit | Pearl | Remember | Platoon | Robber |
| Rough | Repeated | Parrot | Queer | Quiver |
| Reindeer | Quarrel | Panther | Pretty | Quack |

### Words to Remember

**P** Paced, Painting, Pair, Pang, Pansy, Pantaloons, Panther, Pants, Parrot, Party, Pass, Paste, Patch, Peace, Peacock, Pear, Pearl, Penny, People, Pest, Piece, Pigeon, Piglet, Pimple, Place, Plane, Plant, Plastic, Plate, Platoon, Playing, Please, Plenty, Plus, Pond, Pose, Power, Pretty

**Q** Quadrant, Quaint, Quake, Qualify, Quarrel, Quarry, Quarter, Queen, Queer, Quell, Quest, Question, Queue, Quicksand, Quiet, Quilt, Quip, Quit, Quite, Quiver, Quote

**R** Radish, Radish, Rage, Raincoat, Range, Rapid, Rash, Raw, Ray, Reach, Reading, Real, Rectangle, Regal, Regular, Reins, Relish, Remark, Remember, Remind, Repair, Report, Respect, Reward, Riding, Right, River, Robbery, Rocket, Route, Rumour, Running

Date: _____                               Teacher's Signature: _____

# S, T AND U

1. Look at the picture and choose the right spellings:

a.  Schile
    Shale
    Shell

b.  Train
    Trine
    Trayne

c.  Umberela
    Umberalla
    Umbrella

d.  Toeth
    Teath
    Teeth
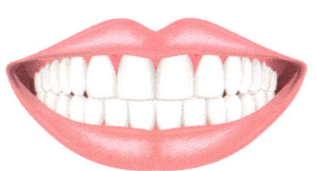

e.  Unicorn
    Uniqorn
    Unicorne

f.  Smake
    Smoke
    Smuk

g.  Stomp
    Stump
    Stamp

h.  Teacher
    Teecher
    Teicher

i.  Stare
    Stair
    Steir
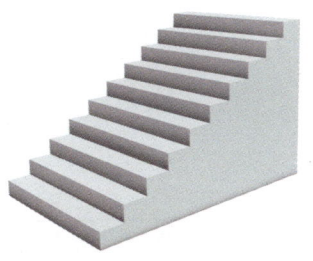

j.  Toust
    Toste
    Toast

Teacher's Signature: _____   Date: _____

2. Solve the crossword with the help of the hints given below:

**Across**
1. Very bad to look at.
2. A passage underground.
3. Opposite direction to North.
7. To minus one number from another.
8. To work hard to achieve something.
9. Below something.
10. A place where we study.
11. To annoy someone.
12. To turn from side to side.

**Down**
1. Opposite of useless.
2. The archer focused on the _____ in front of her.
4. One of a kind.
5. Fifth day of the week.
6. A figure made of straw to keep away birds from fields.
9. He did not let me _____ a word or speak.

3. Write down the names of:
   a. Two days beginning with S: _____ ; _____
   b. Two numbers beginning with T: _____ ; _____

Date: _____                    Teacher's Signature: _____

4. Match the following to make compound words:

a. Time                            stand

b. Some                          mark

c. Under                         gaze

d. Tooth                         thing

e. Stair                           aware

f. Star                             table

g. Un                              pick

h. Trade                         case

5. Solve the jumble and fill in the blanks:

a. July is the _____ month of the year. (esnvhte)

b. Put the glass on the _____. (atlbe)

c. My fathers' brother is my _____. (nulce)

d. The _____ are shining in the night. (tsras)

e. I am _____ I broke your pencil. (osrry)

### Words to Remember

**S** — Saturday, Save, Savour, Saw, Scale, Scarecrow, September, Seventh, Shape, Shell, Ship, Shopping, Shoulder, Simple, Single, Smile, Smoke, Snug, Soak, Soap, Something, Sometime, Sorry, Sort, Spelling, Spiral, Spray, Square, Stars, Stir, Story, Stray, Streak, Style, Sunday, Swing

**T** — Table, Tail, Taken, Tale, Tall, Target, Teacher, Teeth, Thief, Thimble, Thing, Thought, Throw, Thump, Tiger, Toad, Toffee, Toothpick, Tower, Trace, Tread, Treat, Trip, Trouble, Try, Tumble, Twelve, Twenty, Twine, Twist

**U** — Ugly, Ultimate, Unaware, Uncle, Under, Understand, Unicorn, Unique, Unit, Upon, Upwards, Urge, Useful, Usher, Utter

Teacher's Signature: _____      Date: _____

# V, W AND X

1. Tick the correct word:
   a. We put flowers in a vase/vest.
   b. The sun sets in the east/west.
   c. Where/which are you going?
   d. We wear woollen/wooden clothes in winter.
   e. Wash/walk carefully on the road.
   f. 'A, E, I, O, U' are wowels/vowels.

2. Write down the names of the following. Remember each word has to begin with a W!
   a. A day of the week:     W _ _ N _ _ D _ _
   b. A season:              W _ _ T _ _
   c. A kind of grain:       W _ _ _ T
   d. A wild animal:         W _ _ F
   e. A colour:              W _ _ _ E

3. Correct the following sentences:
   a. Her dress was made of valvet.
   b. I saw a womin in the shop.
   c. I like reading books viry much.
   d. I have never seen a volcano erupting.
   d. My brother got a blue whisle on his birthday.
   e. I had to get my leg x-reyed.
   f. The whether is very warm.

Date: _____                                    Teacher's Signature: _____

4. Match the following:

a. Xylophone

b. Van

c. Watch

d. Violin

e. X-mas tree

f. Window

**Words to Remember**

 Van, Violin, Vase, Vest, Velvet, Vowels, Vision, Vein, Vain, Vague, Value, Vulture, Vegetable, Volcano, Video, View, Voice, Vote

 Wash, Watch, Window, Winter, West, Wednesday, Wolf, White, Woman, Walk, Warm, Which, Who, Why, Where, Whether, Wander, Wise, Wrong, While, Wing, Whistle, Whisker, Whisper, Whale, Wisdom, Wheat, Weave, Whisk, Weather, Welcome

 X-Mas, Xylophone, X-Ray, Xylem

Teacher's Signature: _____  Date: _____

# Y AND Z

1. Circle and colour the things that are yellow in colour:

Circle and colour the things that are yellow in colour:

a.  _____  BZREA

b.  _____  AYTCH

c.  _____  PIZ

d.  _____  OZO

e.  _____  KYA

f.  _____  GIGZZA

g.  _____  ROZE

Tick the correct words:
a. There are twelve months in a (your/year).
b. We mix (youth/yeast) with flour to make bread.
c. Is this (your/year) book?
d. A (youth/young) cow is called a calf.
e. The day before today was (yesterday/yeasterday).
f. My favourite flowers are (zinnias/zanys).
g. The boy (youlped/yelped) in fear when he saw the scary movie.
h. My mother always adds the lemon (zest/zany) to my lemonade.

Teacher's Signature: _____  Date: _____

4. Fill in the blanks with either Y or Z to find the words:
   a. The noise made by a bee: BU __ __
   b. The part of food that we pour over our rice: GRAV __
   c. When our head spins, we get: DI __ Z __
   d. To look at something: GA __ E
   e. To give money in exchange of something: PA __
   f. A flatbread topped with vegetables and cheese: PI __ __ A
   g. Not sure about something: MA __ BE
   h. To want something very badly: __ EARN

5. Use the the following letters to make as many new words as possible:

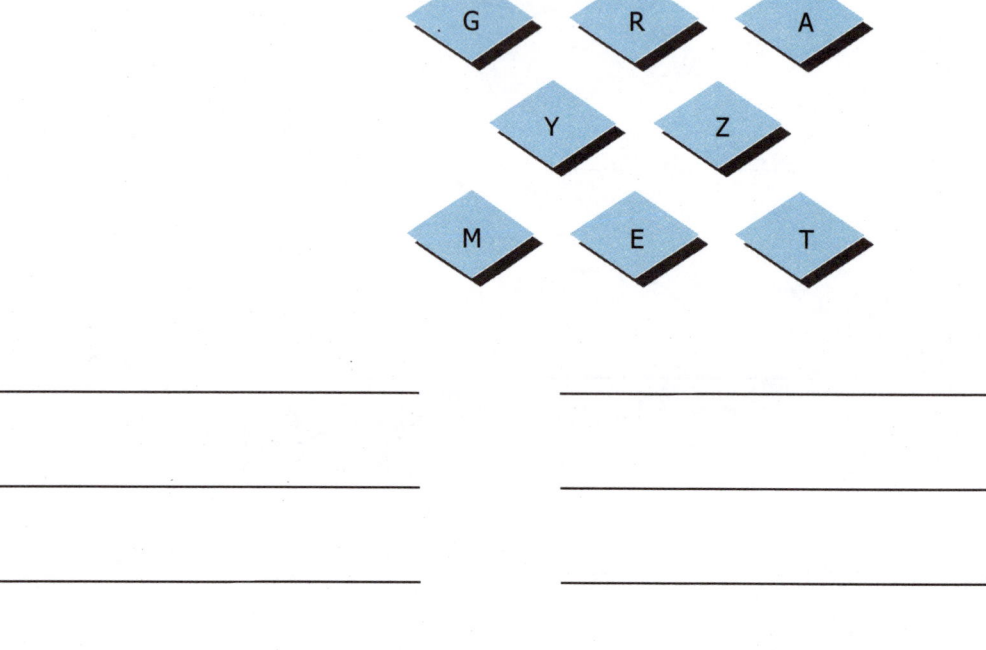

   _____   _____

   _____   _____

   _____   _____

   _____   _____

## Words to Remember

**Y** Yacht, Yardstick, Year, Yearend, Yearn, Yeast, Yellow, Yelp, Yesterday, Yolk, Young, Your, Youth, Youthful, Yummy

**Z** Zany, Zeal, Zebra, Zesty, Zigzag, Zinnia, Zipper, Zone, Zoo, Zucchini

Date: _____   Teacher's Signature: _____

# EXERCISES

Fill in the blanks with the opposites of the words in brackets:
a. It is very (hot) _____ outside.
b. These grapes are very (sour)_____.
c. This cup is (empty) _____.
d. I am feeling (happy)_____ today.
e. I have a (small) _____ bag.

Choose the correct spelling:

a. Oshen/Ochean/Ocean

b. Grandmother/Grendmother/Grandmouther

c. Monkey/ Manky/ Minkey

d. Unfarm/ Uniform/ Unifom

e. Kungaru/Kangaroo/Kengaroo

f. Pilar/Pelor/Pillar

g. Righting/Wrighting/Writing

Teacher's Signature: _____          Date: _____

3. Change the underlined letters to make new words:

   a. FOIL                          __ OIL

   b. PLANK                     PLAN __

   c. TEAR                       TEA __

   d. DREAD                    __ READ

   e. CREAM                   __ REAM

   f. GREASE                 __ REASE

   g. PARTY                    PART __

4. Count and write:

   a. _____

   b. _____

   c. _____

   d. _____

   e. _____

5. Match the words that sound the same:

   a. Sea                       Write

   b. Right                    Wine

   c. Blue                     Vain

   d. Ate                       Sun

   e. Would                See

   f. Son                      Blew

   g. Vein                     Wood

   h. Vine                     Eight

Date: _____                        Teacher's Signature: _____

Circle and correct the wrong spellings:

a. Ship, Truck, Airplane, Car, Scouter

b. Blue, Purple, Green, Penk, Orange

c. Elephant, Lyon, Zebra, Dog, Tiger

d. Run, Sit, Sing, Read, Eit

e. January, Jone, March, July, August

Look at the picture below and correct the mistakes in the paragraph:

Today is Sara's biethday. She has turned eight yours old. Her fiernds have come to her partay. They have all given her meny gifts. They plaed many games and ate the yumy cake. Before going back houme, Sara's friends thanked her mothr. They all had a lot of fan.

# APPENDIX: SIGHT WORDS

Here are some words that we use very often. Learn a new word every day!

| Help | Happy | Around | Basket | Colour | Visitor | Family | Clear |
|------|-------|--------|--------|--------|---------|--------|-------|
| Rain | Watch | Should | Mother | Earth | Food | Grow | Building |
| School | Please | Could | Paper | Paint | Loudly | Welcome | Money |
| Tomorrow | Thank | Children | Thought | Answer | Surprise | Pretty | Mouse |
| Because | Always | Forward | Under | Above | Know | Noise | Start |
| Cream | Study | Sing | Write | People | Water | North | Friend |
| Make | Wasn't | Front | Nothing | Visitor | Found | Hurry | Door |
| Don't | Remember | Isn't | Find | Late | Brown | Time | Only |
| Pushed | Asking | Quiet | Shall | Truth | Working | Awake | Things |
| Learn | Before | Shy | Round | Game | Square | Join | Young |

Date: _____    Teacher's Signature: _____

# ANSWER KEY

## A, B AND C

1. a. Basket    b. Carrot    c. Bicycle    d. Award    e. Bread
   f. Chameleon    g. Anchor    h. Caterpillar    i. Antelope
2. a. black    b. charming    c. amazing    d. constantly    e. burglar
   f. addition
3. a. Bones    b. Children    c. Animals    d. Brothers    e. Aunts
   f. Cherries
4. a. branches    b. circle    c. bamboo    d. basket    e. archer
   f. aching    g. camping
5. a. CATTLE    b. BRAIN    c. FLAG    d. DRAB    e. CURE
   f. AWARE

## D, E AND F

1. a. Dragon    b. Elephant    c. Flamingo    d. Flower    e. Dinosaur
   f. Eighteen    g. Drum    h. Exercise    i. Farming    j. Dream
2. a. Dagger    b. Flame    c. Early    d. Dance    e. English
   f. Force
3. a. Dungeon    b. Eager    c. Forget    d. Factory    e. Elated
   f. Duckling    g. Dodge    h. Escape    i. Famous    j. Frail
4. Do yourself with the help of your teacher/guardian/parents
5. a. deer    b. eyes    c. draw    d. feet    e. Friday
   f. feather    g. energy    h. float    i. dock
   j. emotions
6. Every, One, Very, Eve, Rye, Rove, Ore

## G, H AND I

1. Horse, Golden Eagle, Goat, Hen, Hippopotamus, Giraffe, Goose, Gorilla, Gazelle, Found on a farm: Horse, Goat, Hen, Goose
2. a. I will    b. I am    c. It is    d. I would    e. I have
   f. It will
3. a. Grew    b. Heard    c. Gave    d. Helped    e. Grasped
   f. Got    g. Inferred    h. Greeted    i. Implied
4. a. Grapes and Guavas    b. Igloo    c. Goats, grass

5.

| I | G | L | O | O | G | I | L | T | E | N | G |
|---|---|---|---|---|---|---|---|---|---|---|---|
| H | N | E | I | S | L | A | N | D | T | E | R |
| S | U | J | L | G | T | S | R | L | I | S | O |
| G | E | N | U | I | N | E | G | L | A | E | W |
| E | I | A | P | R | D | O | U | P | I | N | L |
| H | A | S | S | L | E | F | R | E | C | C | D |
| A | O | L | E | H | E | D | G | E | I | I | G |
| H | A | B | I | T | A | B | L | E | C | M | L |
| E | C | H | A | N | K | E | R | E | L | P | E |
| F | G | R | O | C | E | R | Y | K | E | I | A |
| T | G | I | R | A | F | E | F | E | C | S | M |
| Y | G | E | S | T | U | H | E | I | G | H | T |

6. Hungry, into, ice cream, hot, I'll, grumbling, home, got, grateful

# J, K AND L

1. a. Jury    b. Kicked    c. Jukebox    d. Knife    e. January
   f. Kitchen    g. Letter

2. a. keen    b. lucky    c. joking, lottery    d. jazz    e. longer
   f. label

3. a. Dan jumped over the bush.
   b. The rope was tied up in knots.
   c. She is the kindest person I know.
   d. The boys knew how to knit.
   e. Roy bought two loaves of bread.
   f. There were no leaves on the tree.
   g. The tiger is the king of the jungle.
   h. The lawyer presents cases to the judge in court.

4. a. BARK    b. LOVE    c. INJURE    d. PALTRY    e. BANKER
   f. LINK    g. JOKER    h. CHOKE

5. a. Leaves    b. Knives    c. Ladies    d. Jungles    e. Kittens
   f. Jails

# M, N AND O

1. a. MAGICIAN    b. MATHEMATICS    c. OSTRICH    d. NAPKIN    e. OXEN
   f. MONKEY    g. NEIGHBOUR    h. NIGHT

Date: _____    Teacher's Signature: _____

2. a. neighed   b. overheard   c. owl   d. mighty   e. outside
   f. monkeys, noisy            g. owner, neglected

3. a. November   b. money   c. music   d. o'clock   e. nose
   f. orange   g. maximum

4. a. Over — paper
   b. News — paper
   c. Match — stick
   d. Milk — man
   e. Night — time
   f. Mega — phone
   g. Main — land
   h. Note — pad

   (note: lines cross; matches shown: a-time, b-paper, c-stick, d-man, e-come (over-come?), f-phone, g-land, h-pad)

5. a. On   b. Over   c. Near

## Q AND R

1. a. Alpha   b. Acquire   c. Treat   d. Quill   e. Tender
   f. Sport   g. Armour   h. Moral

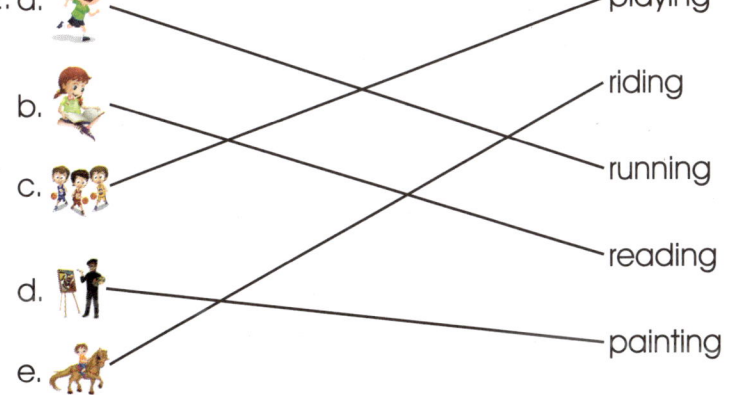

2. a. — running
   b. — reading
   c. — playing
   d. — painting
   e. — riding

3. a. pair   b. pass   c. queue   d. ready   e. people
   f. river   g. plastic   h. quiet   i. quilt   j. reward

4.

| E | D | Q | T | P | A | R | R | O | T |
| L | E | O | Q | U | I | V | E | R | U |
| Q | Q | U | A | C | K | U | I | Q | Q |
| P | P | L | A | T | O | O | N | U | U |
| R | E | P | E | A | T | E | D | A | E |
| E | R | E | M | E | M | B | E | R | E |
| T | O | P | A | N | T | H | E | R | R |
| T | U | R | O | B | B | E | R | E | P |
| Y | G | R | A | P | E | A | R | L | T |
| R | H | E | O | Q | U | I | T | G | O |

## S, T AND U

1. a. Shell   b. Train   c. Umbrella   d. Teeth   e. Unicorn
   f. Smoke   g. Stamp   h. Teacher   i. Stair   j. Toast

2.

Across/Down crossword:
- 1. UGLY
- USEFUL
- 2. TUNNEL
- TARGET
- 3. UOUTH
- 4. UNIQUE
- 5. THURSDAY
- 6. ST(A)RE
- 7. SUBTRACT
- 8. STRUGGLE
- 9. UNDER
- UTTER
- 10. SCHOOL
- 11. TROUBLE
- 12. TWIST

3. a. Seventh   b. Table   c. Uncle   d. Stars   e. Sorry   f. September

4. a. Time — case
   b. Some — thing
   c. Under — stand
   d. Tooth — pick
   e. Stair — gaze
   f. Star — mark
   g. Un — aware
   h. Trade — table

5. a. Saturday, Sunday; b. Ten, twelve, thirteen, twenty, etc.

# W and X

1. a. vase   b. west   c. where   d. woollen   e. Walk   f. vowels
2. a. WEDNESDAY   b. WINTER   c. WHEAT   d. WOLF   e. WHITE
3. a. Her dress was made of velvet.
   b. I saw a woman in the shop.
   c. I like reading books very much.
   d. My brother got a blue whistle on his birthday.
   e. I had to get my leg x-rayed.
   f. The weather is very warm.

4. a. Xylophone
   b. Van
   c. Watch
   d. Violin
   e. X-mas tree
   f. Window

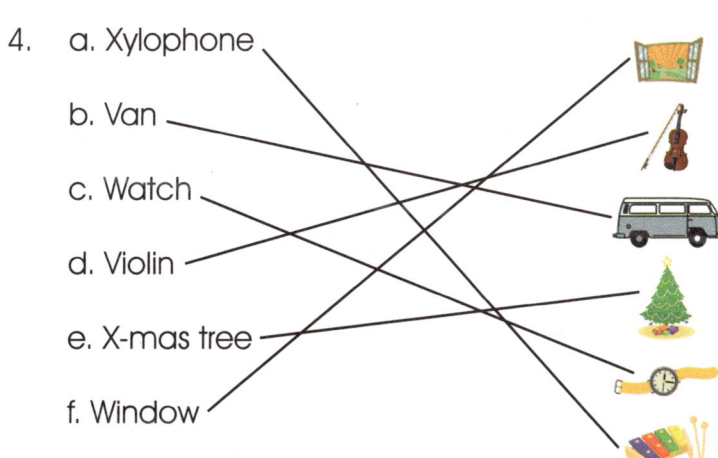

## Y AND Z

1. Circle the following: mango, banana, sun, egg yolk
2. a. ZEBRA   b. YACHT   c. ZIP   d. ZOO   e. YAK
   f. ZIGZAG   g. ZERO
3. a. year   b. yeast   c. your   d. young   e. yesterday
   f. zinnias   g. yelped   h. zest
4. a. BUZZ   b. GRAVY   c. DIZZY   d. GAZE   e. PAY
   f. PIZZA   g. MAYBE   h. YEARN
5. Graze, Gray, Ray, Meat, Met, Mat, Mate, Year, Yet, Rat, Rate, Art, Mart, Gram, Grate, Great, etc.

## EXERCISES

1. a. cold   b. sweet   c. full   d. sad   e. big
2. a. Ocean   b. Grandmother   c. Monkey   d. Uniform   e. Kangaroo
   f. Pillar   g. Writing
3. a. COIL/SOIL/TOIL   b. PLANE/PLANT   c. TEAK/TEAL/TEAM
   d. TREAD/BREAD   e. DREAM   f. CREASE
   g. PARTS
4. a. Five pencils   b. Fifteen dresses   c. Twenty mice
   d. Eleven trees   e. Nine hats
5. a. Sea — See
   b. Right — Write
   c. Blue — Blew
   d. Ate — Eight
   e. Would — Wood
   f. Son — Sun
   g. Vein — Vain
   h. Vine — Wine
6. a. Scooter   b. Pink   c. Lion   d. Eat   e. June
7. Today is Sara's birthday. She has turned eight years old. Her friends have come to her party. They have all given her many gifts. They played many games and ate the yummy cake. Before going back home, Sara's friends thanked her mother. They all had a lot of fun.

Date: _____   Teacher's Signature: _____